trace & write

CURSIVE WRITING

small letters

Published by

MAPLE PRESS PRIVATE LIMITED
Corporate & Editorial Office
A 63, Sector 58, Noida 201 301, U.P., India
phone: +91 120 455 3581, 455 3583
email: info@maplepress.co.in, website: www.maplepress.co.in

2013 Copyright © Maple Press Private Limited

ALL RIGHTS RESERVED. No part of this book may be reproduced or transmitted in any form by any means, electronic or mechanical, including photocopying and recording, or by any information storage and retrieval system, except as may be expressly permitted in writing by the publisher.

Printed in 2024 at Rashtriya Printers, Delhi, India

ISBN: 978-93-50335-91-8

21 20 19 18 17 16 15 14 13 12

aeroplane

ant

apple

alligator axe almonds

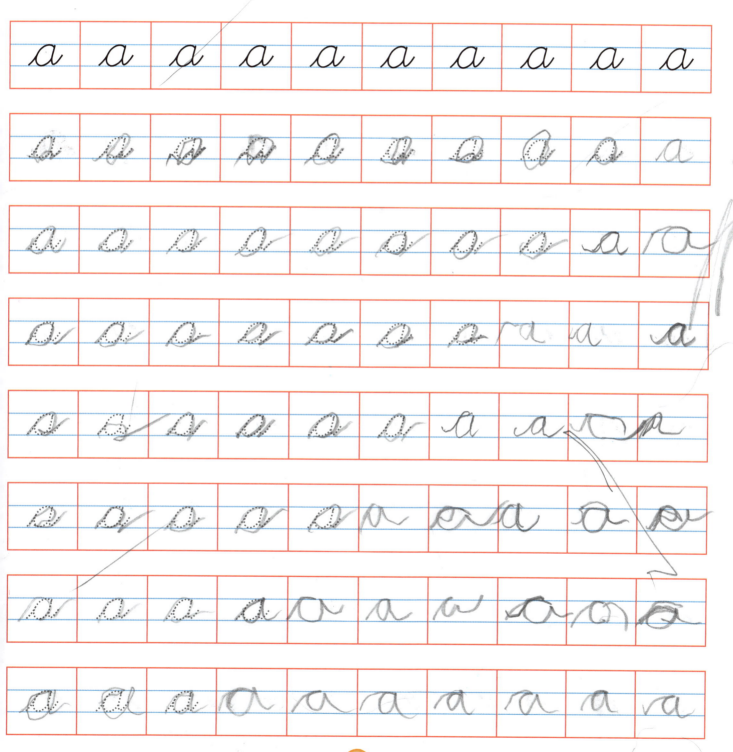

bell   ball   bus

 bee

 banana

 books

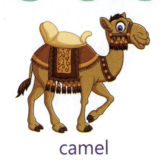 camel
 cat
 candle

cup

cap

crayons

dolphin

dog

doll

duck   door   deer

elephant   earth   egg

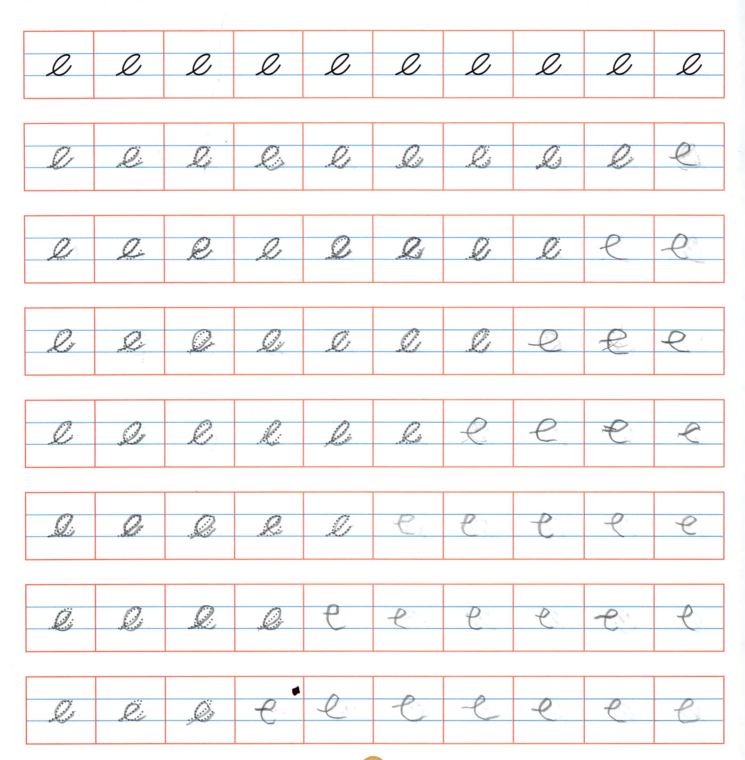

 eagle

 engine

 eraser

fan frog fork

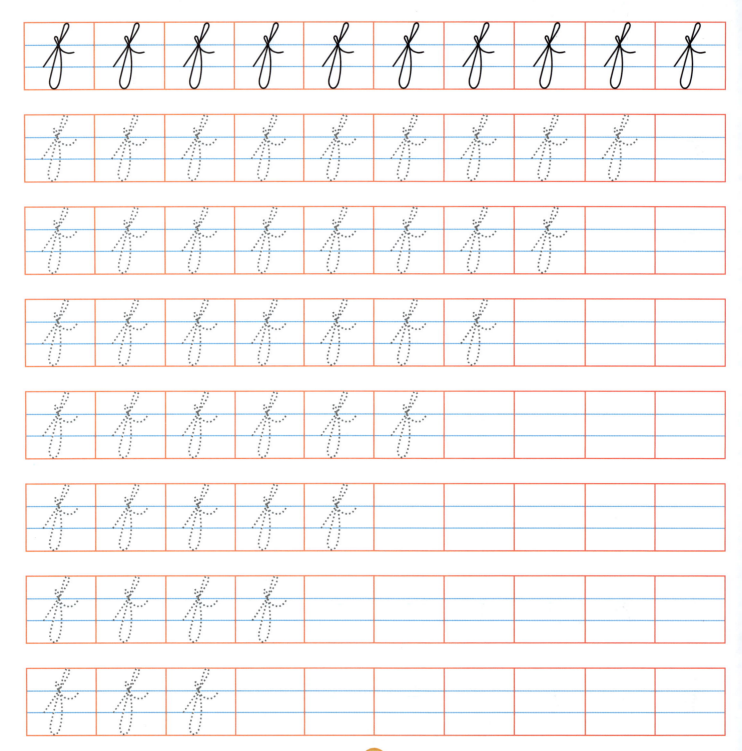

fox

football

flowers

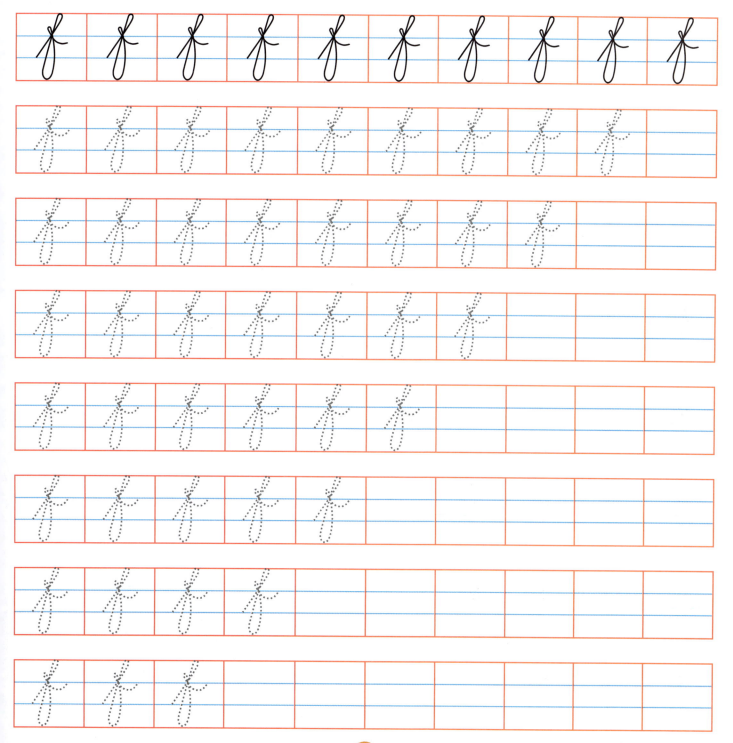

grass   guava   giraffe

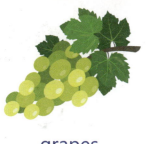  

grapes   goat   guitar

horse   hen   house

igloo inkpot ice-cream

ice cubes

iron

infant

juice

jacket

joker

jaguar

jug

jeep

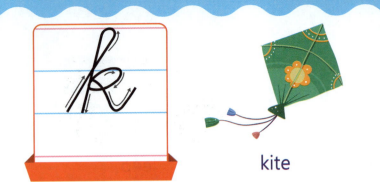

kite   kangaroo   keys

kitten   king   kettle

lion — lemon — lotus

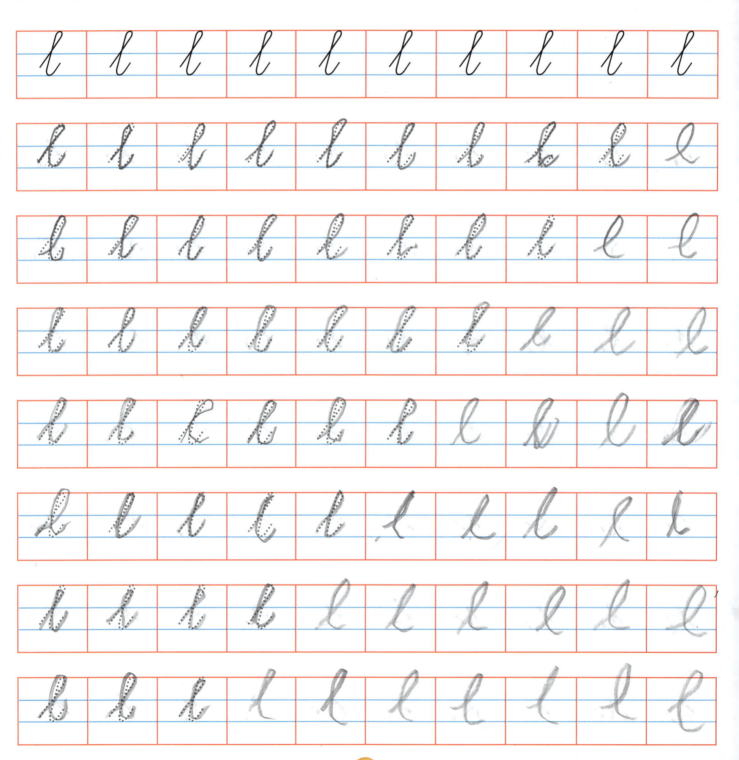

leaf

lock

lamp

mango

mug

monkey

mask

milk

moon

nest　net　nuts

nose

needle

nails

 owl
 orange
 onion

one

octopus

ox

 parrot

 pen

 pear

panda   potato   peacock

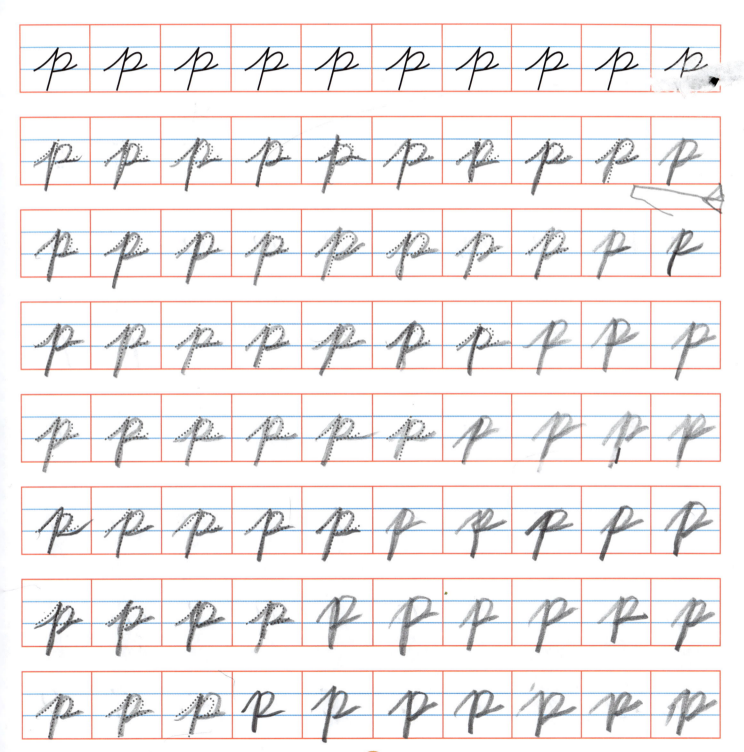

quilts   quill   queen

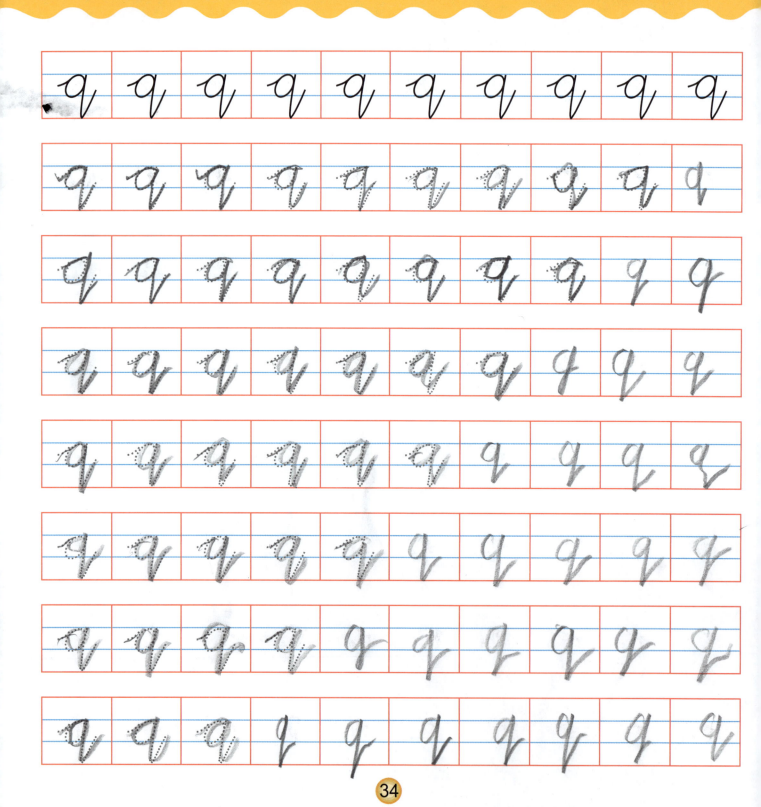

quail

question mark

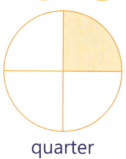
quarter

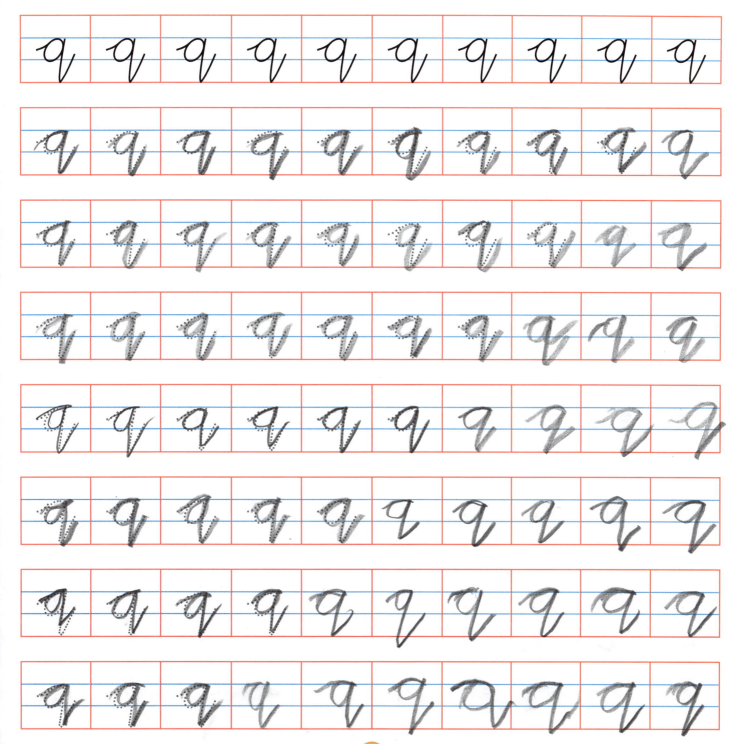

rose

ring

raspberry

rabbit

rock

rainbow

swan sun sunflower

snake

sharpener

ship

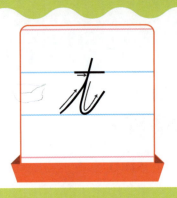
 tiger
 tomato
 table

 turnip
 toothbrush
 toys

 umbrella
 uniform
 urn

unicorn

unicycle

umpire

 van

 vase

 violin

watch

wool

wolf

xenops

x-ray

xylophone

yo-yo　　　yacht　　　yak

zebra

zero

zip

48